Saint Catherine Labouré

Saint Stories

FOR BEGINNING READERS

by Theresa Lincicome Harrell

illustrated by Dianne Lincicome

Printed with Ecclesiastical Permission and Approved for Private or Instructional Use

NIHIL OBSTAT: Deacon Matthew A. Glover,
                             J.D., J.C.L. Censor Librorum

IMPRIMATUR: +Anthony B. Taylor
                             Bishop of Little Rock

April 10, 2024

DEDICATION

This book is lovingly dedicated to Mary Claire and James. We pray you continue to see yourselves in the lives of the saints.

"Truly, I say to you, unless you turn and become like children, you will never enter the kingdom of heaven."
Matthew 18:1-3

Just like you, saints were all small once.

France

This saint was born far away. Her name was Zoe.

Zoe had many brothers and sisters.

She did not get to go to school.

She had to cook and clean for her
family.

Zoe's mother died when she was small.

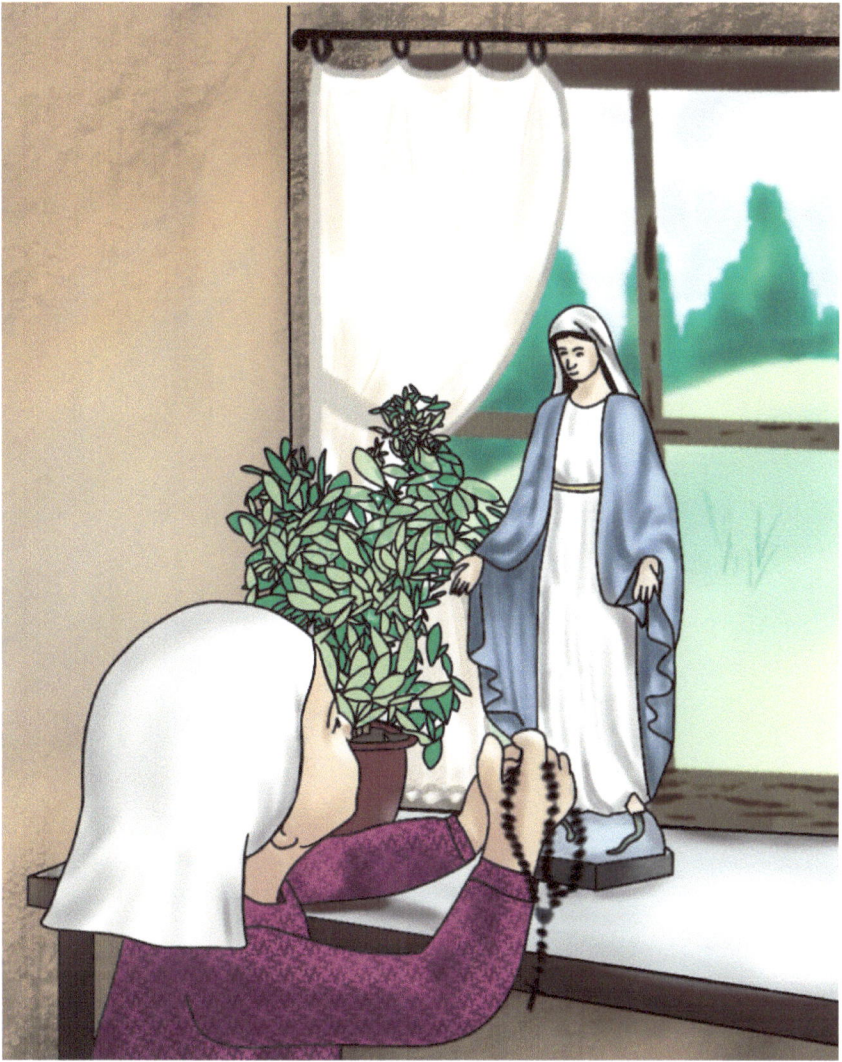

Zoe called Mary her mother for the rest of her life.

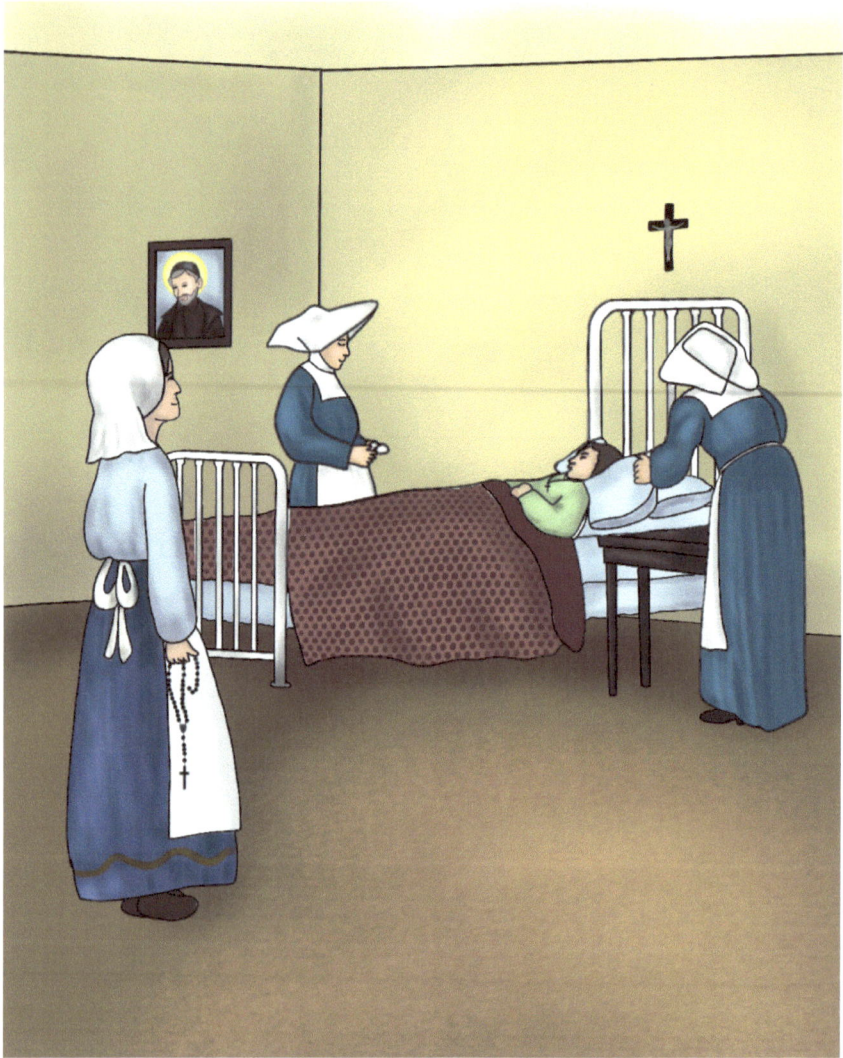

Soon, Zoe wanted to be a nun. Nuns help the poor, old, and sick.

Nuns get a new name. She picked
Catherine!

One night, Catherine woke up. She
heard, "Sister, sister, sister."

Then she saw Mother Mary for the first
time.

She talked to Mary. She rested her
hands on Mary's lap.

Mother Mary often came to her.

Mother Mary asked Catherine to make
her a medal.

Catherine did as Mary asked. Men and women still wear that medal today!

Many are healed because Catherine did as Mother Mary asked.

A blind girl could see after wearing the medal.

A little boy got hurt sledding. He wore the medal and got better.

Catherine went to be with Jesus long ago.

She was named a saint after her death.

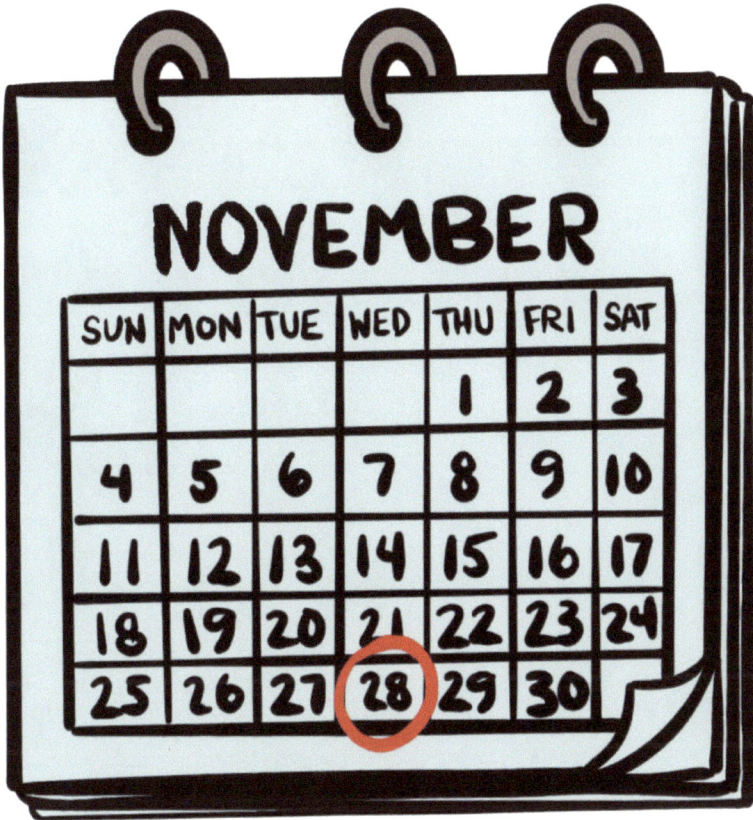

Her feast day is November 28.

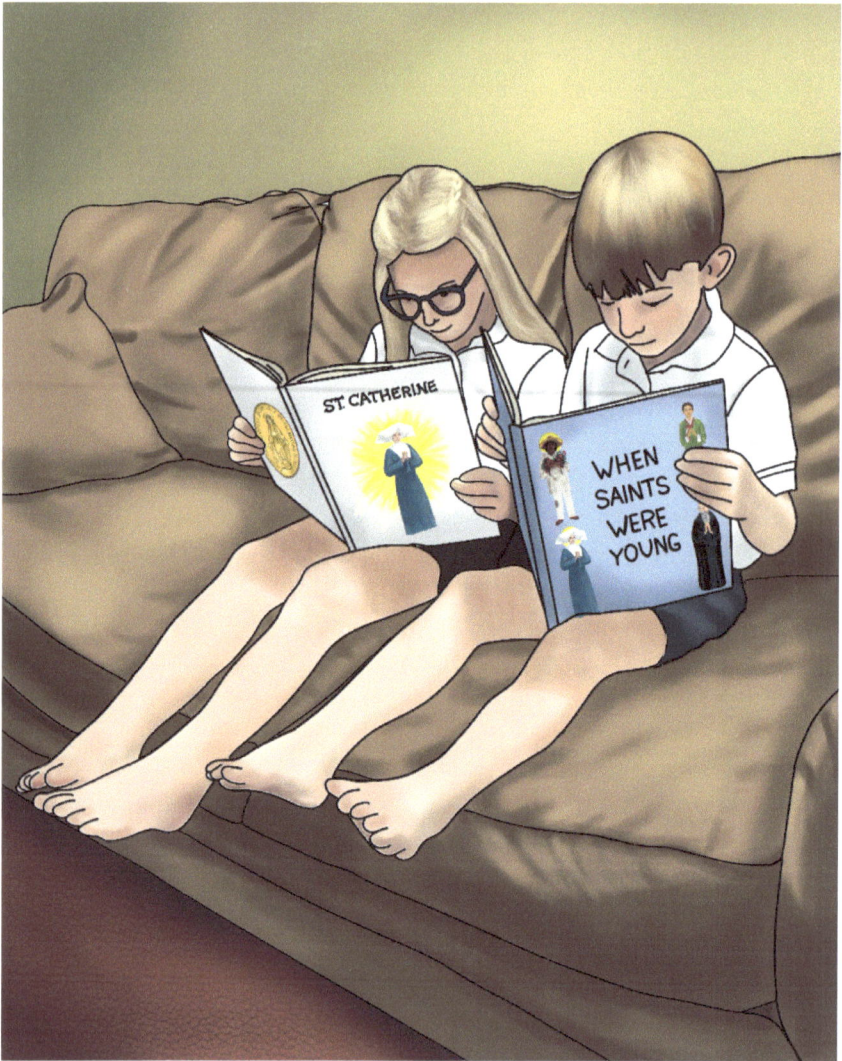

We can learn from Saint Catherine's words.

"One must see God in everyone."

"I tell God everything that is in my heart."

What can you do to be more like St.
Catherine today?

Saint Catherine, pray for us.

All you holy men and women, pray for us.

Can you name the saints?

1-Saint Teresa of Calcutta

2- Saint Catherine Laboure

3- Our Lady of Guadalupe

4- Saint Padre Pio

5- Saint Martin de Porres

6- Saint Kateri Tekakwitha

7- Saint Vincent de Paul

8- Saint Juan Diego

9- Saint Francis of Assisi

10- Saint Patrick

11- Saint Genevieve

12- Saint Benedict

13- Saint Claire of Assisi

14- Saint Agatha Kim

15- Saint Pope John Paul II

16- Saint Gemma Galgani

www.ingramcontent.com/pod-product-compliance
Lightning Source LLC
LaVergne TN
LVHW010024070426
835508LV00001B/42